D0667155

The Celts

sacred symbols

The Celts

Thames and Hudson

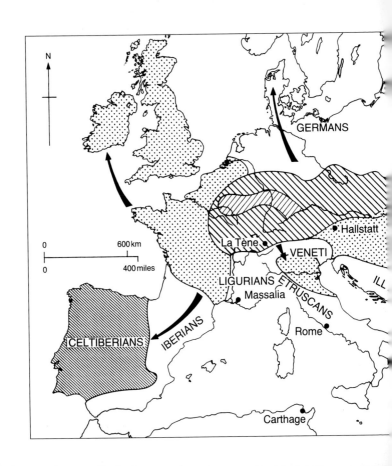

N

600 km
400 miles

GERMANS

Hallstatt

La Tène

VENETI

LIGURIANS

ETRUSCANS

Massalia

ILL

CELTIBERIANS

IBERIANS

Rome

Carthage

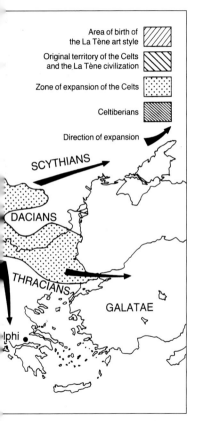

Area of birth of
the La Tène art style

Original territory of the Celts
and the La Tène civilization

Zone of expansion of the Celts

Celtiberians

Direction of expansion

SCYTHIANS

DACIANS

THRACIANS

GALATAE

Iphi ●

Preceding pages Bronze figure, Bouray,
France, 1st century BC – 1st century
AD.

Regions of Europe occupied by the
Celts from 5th century BC to the
Roman conquests of 1st century AD.

For many people the term 'Celtic' conjures up the culture and mythology of the western extremes of Europe – lands steeped in hero-cults and Arthurian romance. This was the view of the Celts promoted by the so-called 'Celtic Revival' of the nineteenth century. But history is more complex: Classical commentators described as 'Celt' a large group of peoples living initially north of the Alps and then spreading eastwards

and southwards. During the thousand years which elapsed before the conversion of the western Celts to Christianity, this warlike people developed a way of life which was highly informed by religious cults and their associated symbolism. For the Celts everything in the natural world possessed its own spirit. And, when Christianity came to them, many pagan deities slipped easily into the characters of the new religion.

THE SACRED

many of the focal points for Celtic
religious ritual and symbolism were
natural sites. Votive offerings have been discovered
in lakes, rivers, marshes and near springs. Hill
regions were often the home for cults devoted to
the worship of mountain gods. Such places, which
also included sacred groves and forest clearings,
might be marked by small shrines or, even more

*characteristically, by phallic standing stones.
These were used to delimit sacred places throughout
the Celtic world and may very well have originated
in attempts to imitate the Sacred Tree. In the sacred
landscape of pre-Celtic Britain, too, sites with
standing stones were clearly designated as places for
religious activity* (below, *the Ring of Brodgar,
Orkney*) — *a legacy for the Celts.*

standing stones

throughout the Celtic lands, from Ireland in the west to
central Europe, sacred places were often marked by the erection
of a wooden or stone pillar. As an expression of vital energy, the
form probably derived from a desire to imitate the tree, an
especially potent symbol for the Celts. Undoubtedly, too, several
such stones were meant to express the brute, primal force
associated with the phallus. They could also serve as landmarks
and foci in the often desolate areas in which they are found.
Sometimes they were elaborately worked and carved, as in the
Turoe stone (opposite) in Co. Galway, Ireland, with
curvilinear motifs typical of Celtic decoration.

the sacred site of Tara

he royal and sacred hill of Tara (opposite) in Co. Meath, Ireland, was a symbol of great significance for the Irish Celts from late Neolithic times to the Christian era. Originally fortified during the Iron Age, the hill became the seat of the kings of Ireland. The site is notable for its two joined ring-forts, in one of which stands the Stone of Fál, which was said to cry out aloud if touched by the rightful king-elect.

According to traditional accounts in Irish mythology, no mortal king could assume true sovereignty at Tara without first coupling with one of the goddesses of the land. The great goddess-queen of Connacht, Medb, is said to have co-habited with nine kings.

mountain goddess

 In Co. Kerry, Ireland, stand two rounded hills (opposite) *known as Dá Chich Anann, or the breasts of Anu, a mother-goddess of the Irish Celts. The fundamental animism of the pagan Celts meant that many cults grew up which attached themselves to specific natural phenomena. Mountains and high places were especial foci of religious activity. Another mountain god was a Celtic form of Jupiter, worshipped especially in the Pyrenees.*

The Celtic mythology of Ireland is rich in traditional tales of magic and taboo, mainly because the country never underwent Romanisation. Anu, frequently confused in legend with Danu or Dana, was a fertility goddess, mother of the Tuatha Dé Danann, the last generation of gods to have ruled the earth.

the well-springs of life

Water, in all its manifestations, fascinated the Celts. A whole universe of myth, ritual and symbolism surrounds sea, lakes, rivers, springs, wells and marshland. Throughout Celtic Europe, from the Bronze Age onwards, votive offerings of fine goods and jewellery, weapons and even human and animal sacrifices were made to lakes, rivers and bogs. The apparently spontaneous movement of water, especially when rising from the ground, must have seemed evidence of supernatural forces at work and curative shrines grew up around important springs and wells. Water from the earth may also have been looked on as a form of contact with the Otherworld.

As in many another time and culture, the Romano-Celtic period saw a large number of cults associated with water gods grow up: a Celtic Neptune at Bath (*above*); three water-goddesses, High Rochester, Northumberland (*opposite*).

The Celtic Tree of Life, drawing by Jen-Delyth.

trees of life and death

The veneration with which the Celts regarded the tree, either singly or in groups, is amply evidenced by the number of shrines devoted to it and its close association with the standing stone, the focal point of many sacred places. Trees could also reflect the joining of lower and upper worlds, their roots burrowing beneath the ground while their branches reached to the sky. The association of trees with hunting is beautifully illustrated in one scene on the Gundestrup Cauldron (see p. 59) (see p. 59) in which a procession is shown carrying a sacred tree, associating it with images of the stag-god. A more sinister and bloody association of trees is described by Tacitus: the Druids often used sacred groves as sites for human sacrifice.

flux and change charac-
terized Celtic life, cus-
toms and religious
symbolism, perhaps a
reflection of the migratory
history of the people.
Everything and everyone
could be represented as
something else; Irish
and Welsh mythology is
full of tales of animals who
were once humans, and gods
in both human and animal

shape. This ambiguity extended to the
representation of all human-like
forms and functions: multi-
headed figures, masks and
head-dresses. And the
final metamorphosis,
death, sometimes ritually
violent in the form of
sacrifice, was regarded as
a minor interruption to a
long life which would
continue to flourish in
the Otherworld.

war-gods
and warriors

I n the cult of the warrior the subtle ambiguities of Celtic
symbolism are very evident. Much of the iconography of
fighting men is also a way of representing the gods,
maintaining the continuity of human and divine. More
strikingly, perhaps, the warriors are not all male, although the
female ones also display the combination of aggression and
sexuality present in images of war-gods, especially in Britain.
A gold coin from Gaul (opposite above) depicts two horses
side by side, one of which bears a triumphant horsewoman,
naked apart from a belt and short cape. In Irish mythology
the goddesses associated with war, Macha, Nemhain,
Morrigán and Reb, were also fertility deities.

Opposite Warriors, some
with animal-crested helmets,
bearing a sacred tree, from
the Gundestrup Cauldron.

Although endowed with war-like associations and qualities, the Celtic female deities of the battlefield do not engage directly in combat themselves. Their function is to influence events which may be achieved by metamorphosis. Morrigán, the Phantom Queen, appears to the Ulster warrior, Cú Chulainn, at various times in the guises of wolf, heifer and eel.

Bronze cult wagon of a warrior,
6th or 7th century BC.

hunters and hunted

There was a very special relationship in Celtic mythology between the hunter and the hunted. The quarry, most notably the stag and the boar, was revered almost as much as the hunter-deity. After all, the death of the beast led to its immortality, and there are many stories in the Celtic vernacular tradition of magical stags and boars luring their pursuers to death and the Otherworld. Other images and figures identify hunter-gods and goddesses with the Classical Diana, especially in Gaul and Britain.

The deeds of Finn, the hero of the Fenian Cycle of Irish myths, and his hunter-warriors, the Fianna, are largely ones of confrontation with the supernatural in the hunt. At the great hunt of the magic boar of Ben Balben in Sligo, Finn refuses the healing water to Diarmaid, his rival in love, after the latter has been wounded by the boar.

mother-goddesses

*abundance and fecundity were central concerns of all
ancient societies, and the Celts were no exception. The idea
of an all-providing mother figure found constant expression
throughout the Celtic lands in image and in legend. Often
such goddesses were depicted in groups of three (the most
sacred and potent number for the Celts) and surrounded by
symbols of plenty – fruit, bread and corn; sometimes one of
the three figures would be shown holding a baby. They were
also closely associated with sacred sources, from small
springs to great thermal baths, as at Aquae Sulis (Bath)
where they were known as the 'Suleviae'. The Irish
goddesses of fertility were often identical to those of war, like
Medb, who granted her favours to nine successive kings.*

Opposite Triple
mother-goddess,
Vertault, Burgundy.

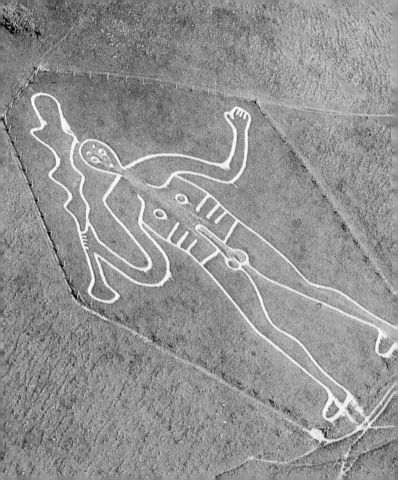

phallus

If the triple goddess represented the female principle of fecundity, then the phallus was certainly the most potent symbol of the male principle. And like most other Celtic symbols it had both divine and human connotations. War-gods were sometimes represented with erect phalli, which drew attention to their sexual potency and their association – like their female counterparts – with the fertility of the earth. The famous chalk giant (opposite) of Cerne Abbas, Dorset, is shown brandishing a huge club, yet was almost certainly at the centre of local fertility rites. Another level of significance: this figure may also have represented Hercules.

On the Celtic festival of Beltene (1 May) the villagers of Cerne Abbas would dance around a maypole erected 70 feet further up the hill than the giant's head – a fertility ritual still practised in the early part of this century.

heads ...

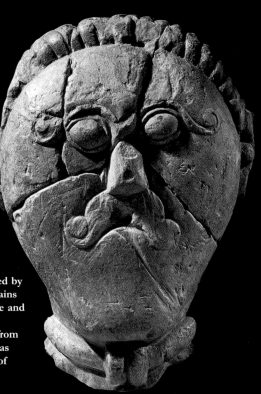

The severed head could also be a lethal weapon. Conohobar, mythical king of Ulster and first of the nine consorts of the goddess-queen Medb, was killed by a brain-ball (brains mixed with lime and then allowed to harden) made from the head of Meas Geaghra, king of Leinster.

... and head-hunters

One of the most shocking characteristics of the Celts for Classical commentators was that they were – at least in battle – head-hunters. The warrior who decapitated his enemy had more than proof of victory: he was also possessing himself of the sacred and protective powers supposed to reside within the human head. Skulls were frequently positioned at the doors of Celtic temples to act as spiritual guardians. Gods were depicted with over-large heads, while especial importance was attached to the janiform head, because of its ability to look in both directions at once. A famous example from Roquepertuse in the south of France shows the human and the divine, the warrior and the war-god, gripped in the bill of a goose (see pp. 20–21).

Opposite Stone head, 3rd or 2nd century BC, found in Bohemia.

the triple head

the number 'three' held deeply auspicious connotations for the Celts, certainly in Germany, Gaul and Britain. Of all the elements of Celtic iconography, it was the human head – symbol of spiritual potency – which was a subject of 'triplism'. In traditional Celtic literature the presence and repetition of the number 'three' had the effect of strengthening and intensification. The mother-goddess, for instance, was often represented in groups of three. But even in single-figure representations of gods or of their heads, it was not uncommon to find them given three faces – one main and two subsidiary.

Opposite Three-headed god on a terra-cotta vase, Bavay, France, 2nd century BC.

the transformed head

masks and head-dresses are often associated with the religious rituals and symbolism of the Celts. Although information about ceremonial is far from plentiful, archaeological evidence does seem to point to the wearing of special headgear during religious ceremonies. This could take the form of bronze diadems or chain head-dresses to be worn over a leather helmet. Crowns were sometimes adorned with small reproductions of the human face, but relatively few full-scale masks have been found. These probably symbolized the metamorphosis of the priest into a superior being, to be held in front of the face during a procession to represent some deity.

Opposite Mask on a bronze flagon, Kleinaspergle, Germany, 5th century BC.

There is a fascinating story of metamorphosis in The Mabinogion. Groydion, a magician, provokes a war by sorcery between his uncle Math and Pryderi, the lord of Dyfed, so that his brother Gilfaethwy can seduce Math's virgin servant Goewin. On hearing of this deviousness, Math summons up his own magic, causing his two nephews to be turned into a stag and hind for one year, a boar and crow for the second and male and female wolves for the third.

the divine beast

the interchangeability of deity, man and beast is a constant theme of Celtic iconography. Cernunnos, lord of the animals and of plenty, appears with the antlers of a stag; he is also closely associated with the snake, a symbol of renewal. Caer, the beloved of love-god Oenghus, changes into swan-form every alternate year.

Opposite A human-headed horse, detail from a bronze wine flagon, Reinheine, Germany, 5th–4th century BC.

the ultimate sacrifice

again, *most of the bloodier details of the sacrificial practices of the Celts come from Classical commentaries. Lucan refers to a sacred wood in the region of Marseilles, where every tree was smeared with the blood of victims. In Anglesey, according to Tacitus, there was a grove with altars covered with the grisly remains of druidical death ceremonies. Another favoured method of human sacrifice was the burning alive of the victim within a huge wicker cage – the 'wicker man'. Virtually all varieties of animal were sacrificed, although there does seem to have been a preference for boars, which were sometimes ritually buried whole. Yet, sacrifice – the ultimate metamorphosis from life to death – was also the key to instant rebirth in the agelessness of the Otherworld.*

Opposite One interpretation of this scene from the Gundestrup Cauldron is that the smaller figure is a sacrifice being pushed into a shaft.

SYMBOLIC

although *animal sacrifice was rife in the Celtic world, both wild and domestic beasts were highly revered. And because Celtic religious belief was based very much upon the natural world, we find great flexibility in animal representation – gods who are part beast, part human, and certain species which are clearly intended to be supernatural. Stags*

BEASTS

for their virility, boars for their aggression, and horses for their grace and strength, seem to have been particularly favoured symbols. Closer to domestic life, the bull and dog were also treated with reverence.

The complete expression of the god-like qualities of the horse: a carving on a hillside at Uffington, Oxfordshire, possibly the tribal symbol of the Atrebates, expressing here protection of the tribe and its lands.

boar

The wild boar is ubiquitous in Celtic iconography and mythology. Dorsal bristles raised in blatant aggression, it appeared on coins, trumpets and helmet crests from England to Hungary and Romania. Its ferocity made it a natural warrior symbol, but its full significance was much greater: it was also the most common quarry of the Celtic hunter. As such, it enjoyed a special symbolic relationship with hunter-gods; Archinna, the huntress deity of the Ardennes, is represented, dagger in hand, astride a wild boar.

Again, the boar was associated with feasting and festivity, since its meat was particularly prized.

Bronze boar, Hungary,
2nd century BC.

bull

aggression and
strength were reckoned high
virtues by the warrior Celts,
qualities associated with their
most potent animal symbols.
The untamed bull was venerated in
all the parts of Europe settled by
the Celts, although its warlike
connotations were tempered by the
symbolism – that of agricultural plenty – associated with its
domestic counterpart, the ox. The bull also seems to have been a
symbol of fertility; there are records of the sacrifice of white bulls
by Druids during fertility rites.

Above Bronze bull, Blansko, Czechoslovakia, 6th century BC.

dog

dogs had three main areas of symbolic association for the Celts: hunting, healing and death. The healing connotation is especially intriguing: it was believed that cures for certain ailments could be effected by the application of canine saliva. The association with the hunt is an obvious one: dogs are depicted throughout Celtic Europe in the company of both hunters and huntresses, whom they aided in the pursuit of quarry and also protected. The Dutch goddess, Nehalennia, a popular deity worshipped on the coast, is often shown with an especially friendly-looking dog, who is clearly playing the role of protector. The connection with death is clearly a reference to canine presences in the Otherworld; *The Mabinogion* relates that Arawn, a god of the underworld, was accompanied by a pack of white dogs with red ears.

Opposite Canine figure from *The Book of Durrow*, 7th century AD.

horse

Symbol of speed, beauty and sexual prowess, the horse also had powerful religious connotations for the Celts. Sacred images of horses abound in their art, from hill figures to stone carvings. The animal was closely associated with the Celtic sun-god, who is often depicted on horse-back on the stone columns of Gaul and western Germany. But the most famous Celtic horse deity was the fertility goddess Epona, patroness of cavalry officers; Iron Age coins also show images of horsewomen and female charioteers. So many Celtic cults had associations with the horse that it is probable that it was held in high reverence because of its innate qualities.

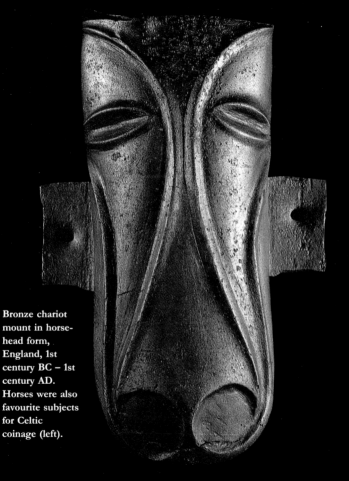

Bronze chariot mount in horse-head form, England, 1st century BC – 1st century AD. Horses were also favourite subjects for Celtic coinage (left).

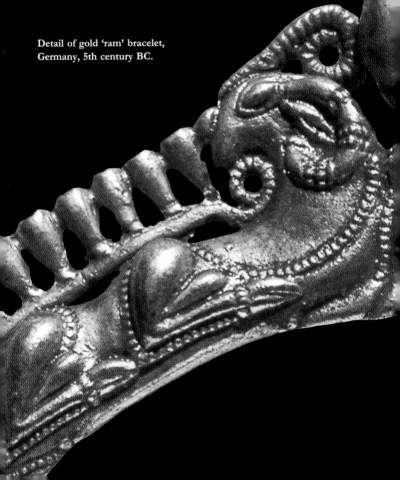

Detail of gold 'ram' bracelet,
Germany, 5th century BC.

ram

Yet another symbolic beast associated with the Celts' admiration of animal strength and aggression, the ram enjoyed cult status during the Romano-Celtic period, especially in Gaul and Britain. There, it was associated with the Roman god Mercury, an association which derived directly from Classical mythology. But there is good reason to believe that the ram had a more purely warlike meaning for the Celts, since it was sometimes represented in the company of a war god. A curious variant on ram symbolism was the ram-headed serpent, another example of the ambiguity and flexibility of Celtic thought. This strange hybrid, often shown in the company of the antlered god Cernunnos, combined the symbolism of fertility and aggression of the ram with the snake's association with both the underworld and renewal.

stag

The Horned One, Cernunnos, Lord of All the Stags, was one of the most potent of all the Celtic zoomorphic gods. He is shown on one of the plates of the Gundestrup Cauldron (opposite), seated in splendour, surrounded by symbols of fertility and plenty, accompanied by a stag and a ram-horned serpent. The symbolism of the stag went beyond obvious maleness and aggressive qualities; the spreading antlers associated the king of the forest with the trees because of the similarity to branch growth. And, like deciduous species of tree, the shedding of antlers in spring and autumn also made the stag the embodiment of the cyclical growth-decay-growth of nature. With the boar, the stag was the most prized quarry of hunters.

eagle

another Celtic nature symbol which had strong Roman affiliations was the eagle, emblem of Jupiter, god of the skies. During the Romano-Celtic period the sun god of the Celts became merged with the Roman deity and took on the same associations, including that of the eagle. The magnificent wingspan of the bird and its ability to fly at great heights made it a natural companion for any deity of the heavens. In The Mabinogion, *Lleu*, a divine warrior, whose name means 'Bright One of the Skilful Hand', is struck a fatal blow, but immediately changes into an eagle and flies into an oak tree, the sacred tree of Jupiter.

Opposite Eagle and horse, two sacred beasts, on a Celtic coin.

THE SPIRIT

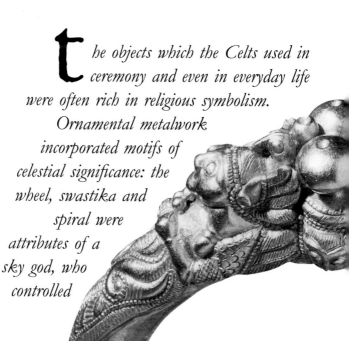

*t*he objects which the Celts used in ceremony and even in everyday life were often rich in religious symbolism. Ornamental metalwork incorporated motifs of celestial significance: the wheel, swastika and spiral were attributes of a sky god, who controlled

sun and lightning. The torc symbolized authority and often accompanied representations of gods. Cauldrons were especially prized and sometimes enjoyed the status of cult object within a tribe; Irish myths tell of cauldrons of abundance, which seems to indicate their use in ritual feasting.

Gold arm-ring, Germany, *c.* 4th century BC.

boat

ritual and symbolism associated with boats was common among all the Celtic tribes of north-west Europe. Model boats in precious metals were made as offerings to the gods, especially those directly connected with the sea and water. A sea passage may also have suggested the journey of the soul to the Otherworld. Manannán Mac Liv, an Irish sea god with powers of magic and illusion, rode the waves like Poseidon in a horse-drawn chariot and carried Celtic heroes to the Otherworld beneath the sea.

A tiny gold boat (*opposite*) of the first century BC,
part of a larger hoard of precious objects, was
found at Broighter, Co, Derry, Northern Ireland.
It comes complete with seven oars.

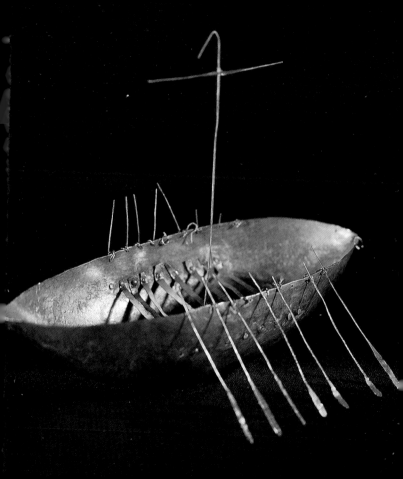

the cauldron of rebirth

Ceremonial cooking vessels were central to the ceremonies of the Otherworld, the feasting associated with rebirth and resurrection. References to magic cauldrons abound in Celtic literature; one tale has it that the Irish possessed a cauldron into which their dead soldiers were thrown, then cooked at night to rise and fight again the next day. The Gundestrup Cauldron (this page and opposite), found in a peat bog in Jutland, depicts a mythological narrative involving a wide range of gods and icons, including a bearded god, served by two acolytes and the solar wheel god, with mythical beasts in attendance.

The Gundestrup Cauldron, Denmark, 3rd–4th century BC, made of decorated silver, may originally have been taken from Gaul to Denmark.

fire

f *or the chilly lands of northern Europe fire held a very special significance: it pushed back the outer darkness and brought warmth to tribal settlements. Ritual bonfires were lit to mark special occasions in the Celtic calendar such as Beltene (1 May) and Samhain (1 November). Midsummer was also marked in both pagan and Christian periods by fire festivals. A more sinister use of fire by the Celts was noted by several Classical commentators, including Julius Caesar. As senior holy men, the Druids were responsible for public sacrifice to the gods; their victims were sometimes imprisoned in huge human-form wicker cages which were then set alight.*

Opposite A scene from the film, *The Wicker Man (1973).*

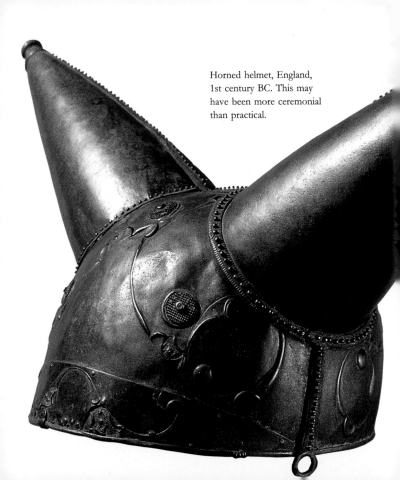

Horned helmet, England, 1st century BC. This may have been more ceremonial than practical.

helmet

for such a warlike people as the Celts, the weapons and accoutrements of the battlefield were obvious objects for veneration. Valuable military equipment was sometimes cast into water or marsh as a votive offering to the gods. It is likely, too, that some warriors were buried with their full regalia and helmets of bronze and of iron with bronze decoration have been found in soldiers' graves. The helmet was itself a special object of significance and symbolism, presumably because of the high status accorded to the human head by the Celts. There are a number of examples in Celtic imagery of horned helmets, another way perhaps of representing deities in human form with horns.

the s-shape

the elaborate twists and intertwinings of late Celtic art are only the most refined expression of a fascination with spirals which goes back through the whole history of the Celts. In pagan times spiral and S-shaped symbols were associated with sky and solar cults. The solar god himself was sometimes represented carrying S-shaped objects, perhaps intended to represent lightning bolts.

Enamelled bronze brooch,
England, 1st century AD.

swastika

One of the great enduring symbols of
the whole of the Ancient World, the
swastika had wide currency as a sign of
good luck and of solar beneficence. The
motif occurs throughout the lands occupied
by the Celts, sometimes on stonework in
the company of images of the spoked
wheel, another powerful sun symbol.

torc

One of the most magnificent figures of the
Gundestrup Cauldron is that of the Horned One,
Cernunnos, with his branching antlers. Around his
neck he wears a torc and carries another. Other Celtic
deities were depicted wearing or carrying torcs, almost
certainly because this was a symbol of dignity and
status. Important people were buried with torcs, and
hoards of buried torcs and coins have been found,
probably buried as offerings to some deity.

Opposite Gold torc, England, 1st century AD.

wheel

traditionally a religious icon in northern
Europe, by Romano-Celtic times the spoked
wheel had become a specific symbol of the sun
and the solar deities. Model wheels have been
found in graves, presumably buried with the dead
to help illuminate their journey to the
Otherworld. Certain cults also threw miniature
wheels into rivers and lakes as offerings to the
gods. The Celtic version of Jupiter was especially
associated with the wheel; shrines devoted to his
worship sometimes also incorporate swastikas.

Opposite Detail from the Gundestrup Cauldron.

THE CHRISTIAN

t he massive movement of northern European people in the immediate post-Roman period effectively redrew the boundaries of the Celtic sphere of influence. Germanic people pushing westward across Europe eventually confined Celtic culture to the seaboard edges. During this period, too,

CELTS

Christianity spread among the Celtic tribes, especially in Ireland, inspiring a great flowering of the decorative arts. But the traditional motifs still recurred in manuscripts (below) inspired by the new religion. The ageless symbols of the Celts passed painlessly into the iconography of the new religion.

cross

even in pre-Christian times the Celts had used the cross as a religious symbol. As in many other aspects of belief, the iconography and practice of the Christian church fitted easily with the pagan past – the cross could now take its place as a central motif in Celtic art. In Ireland, especially, the Christian era saw the great flowering of stone cross making. The traditional Celtic skills of metalworking and jewellery were also put at the service of the new faith: this twelfth-century oak and bronze cross (opposite) was made for Turlough O Conna, High King of Ireland, to hold a relic of the True Cross.

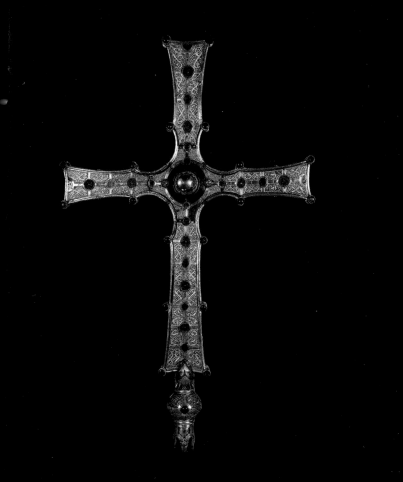

shrine

although the Celts often chose natural places for religious activity – the sacred groves of druidical sacrifice – they also built structures, usually of great simplicity, for the same purpose. Such places were not venues for communal worship – any such activity would take place in the area outside – but rather foci for very specific ceremonies. For instance, the remains of offerings of weapon hoards and even animals have been found at shrine sites. This intense concentration of religious and symbolic experience in very specific places and objects continued unbroken among the western Celts into the Christian era.

Opposite Detail of the Stowe Missal Shrine, a bronze box, Ireland, 11th century AD.

a celtic 'carpet'

*t*he use of pagan motif and symbolism for the
Christian cause achieved one of its high points in the
so-called 'carpet' pages of The Book of Durrow
(opposite). Traditional Celtic interlace, trefoil designs
and knots accompany other pages of symbolic
representations of the four Evangelists, although the
imagery of both men and animals is non-naturalistic,
very much in the mode of earlier, non-Christian art.
There is also a striking resemblance on the 'carpet'
pages to the patterns of earlier Celtic metalwork.

the book of Kells

Probably the greatest artistic achievement of the Celtic world,
The Book of Kells (c. AD 800) is a mine of complex
symbolism. There are the Christian symbols for the four
evangelists: the Man for Matthew, the Lion for Mark, the Calf
for Luke and the Eagle for John, which are represented
throughout the manuscript. But intertwined with this imagery
are distinctively Celtic motifs; the rosette, symbol of the sun,
spirals, knots and interlacing. Animal symbolism, too, is
introduced at every possible opportunity: fish, cats, mice, hens,
snakes, dragons and birds.

Sources of Illustrations

Photo Aerofilms 13; National Museum, Budapest 42; Musée de Chatillon sur Seine (photo Jean Roubier) 27; Nationalmuseet, Copenhagen 39, 51, 58, 59, 69; drawing Jen-Delyth 18; Dublin: National Museum of Ireland 57, 73, 74, Courtesy Board of Trinity College 45, 70–71, 77, 78, 79; photo Werner Forman Archive 10; British Museum, London 4, 47, 62, 64, 66, 68; Musée Borély, Marseilles 20–21; photo George Mott 14; Prähistorische Staatssammlung, Munich 46; Museum of Antiquities, Newcastle 17; Bibliothèque Nationale de France, Paris 33, (Cabinet des Médailles) 23 above, 52; National Musuem, Prague 30; Landesmuseum für Vor-und Frühgeschichte, Saarbrücken 36, 54–55; Musée des Antiquités Nationales, St-Germain-en-Laye (photo © RMN) 2, 24; Historisches Museum der Pfalz, Speyer 48; Württembergisches Landesmuseum, Stuttgart 34; photo Homer Sykes 8–9; photo Telegraph Colour Library 40–41; Naturhistorisches Museum, Vienna 43.

Any copy of this book issued by the publisher as a paperback is sold subject to the condition that it shall not by way of trade or otherwise be lent, resold, hired out or otherwise circulated without the publisher's prior consent in any form of binding or cover other than that in which it is published and without a similar condition including these words being imposed on a subsequent purchaser.

© 1995 Thames and Hudson Ltd, London

First published in the United States of America in 1995 by Thames and Hudson Inc., 500 Fifth Avenue, New York, New York 10110

Library of Congress Catalog Card Number 95-60475
ISBN 0-500-06014-2

All Rights Reserved. No part of this publication may be reproduced or transmitted in any form or by any means, electronic or mechanical, including photocopy, recording or any other information storage and retrieval system, without prior permission in writing from the publisher.

Printed and bound in Slovenia by Mladinska Knjiga